This New Puppy Journal Belongs To:

_____

A True Friend...
  Leaves Paw Prints On Your Heart

How Our Story Began

Insert Photo Here

I Brought You Home On:_____

The First Thing You Did Was:_____

_____

I Named You:_____

Your Puppy Profile

Actual Birthday:
_____

Adoption Day:
_____

Shelter/Breeder:
_____

    Name:
_____

    Phone:
_____

License Number:
_____

Rabies Tag Number:
_____

Microchip Information:
_____

    Chip #
_____

    Phone:
_____

Gender:
_____

Spay/Neutered:
_____

Eye Color:
_____

Coat Color:
_____

Other Important Notes:
_____

_____

_____

_____

Pet Insurance Information

Company:

Website:

Address:

Phone:

Deductible:

Services Covered:

☐ Annual Visits

☐ Emergency

Annual Maximum:

Other Important Notes:

Vet Information

Office Name:
_____

Preferred Doctor:
_____

Address:
_____

_____

_____

Phone:
_____

After Hours Contact:
_____

Cell Phone:
_____

Website:
_____

Other Important Information:
_____

_____

_____

_____

_____

_____

_____

_____

Vaccination Record

Date	Age	Vaccine	Mfg.	Lot#	Given By"

Vaccination Record

Date	Age	Vaccine	Mfg.	Lot#	Given By"

Vaccination Record

Date	Age	Vaccine	Mfg.	Lot#	Given By"

Vaccination Record

Date	Age	Vaccine	Mfg.	Lot#	Given By"

Vaccination Record

Date	Age	Vaccine	Mfg.	Lot#	Given By"

Groomer Information

Groomer Name:
_____

Address:
_____

_____

_____

Phone:
_____

Website:
_____

Other Important Information:
_____

_____

_____

_____

_____

_____

_____

_____

_____

_____

_____

Remember When...

My New Puppy Journal

_____

_____

_____

_____

_____

_____

_____

_____

_____

_____

_____

_____

_____

_____

_____

_____

_____

_____

Remember When...

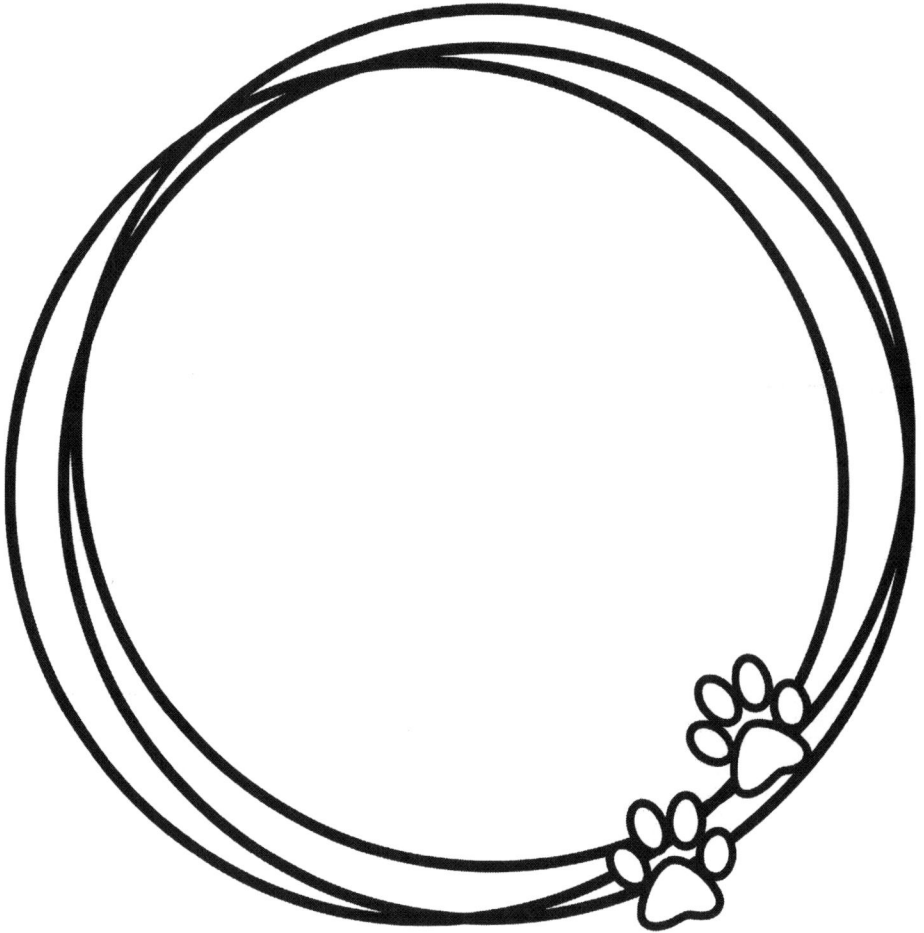

My New Puppy Journal

_____

_____

_____

_____

_____

_____

_____

_____

_____

_____

_____

_____

_____

_____

_____

_____

_____

Remember When...

My New Puppy Journal

_____

_____

_____

_____

_____

_____

_____

_____

_____

_____

_____

_____

_____

_____

_____

_____

_____

Remember When...

My New Puppy Journal

_____

_____

_____

_____

_____

_____

_____

_____

_____

_____

_____

_____

_____

_____

_____

_____

_____

Remember When...

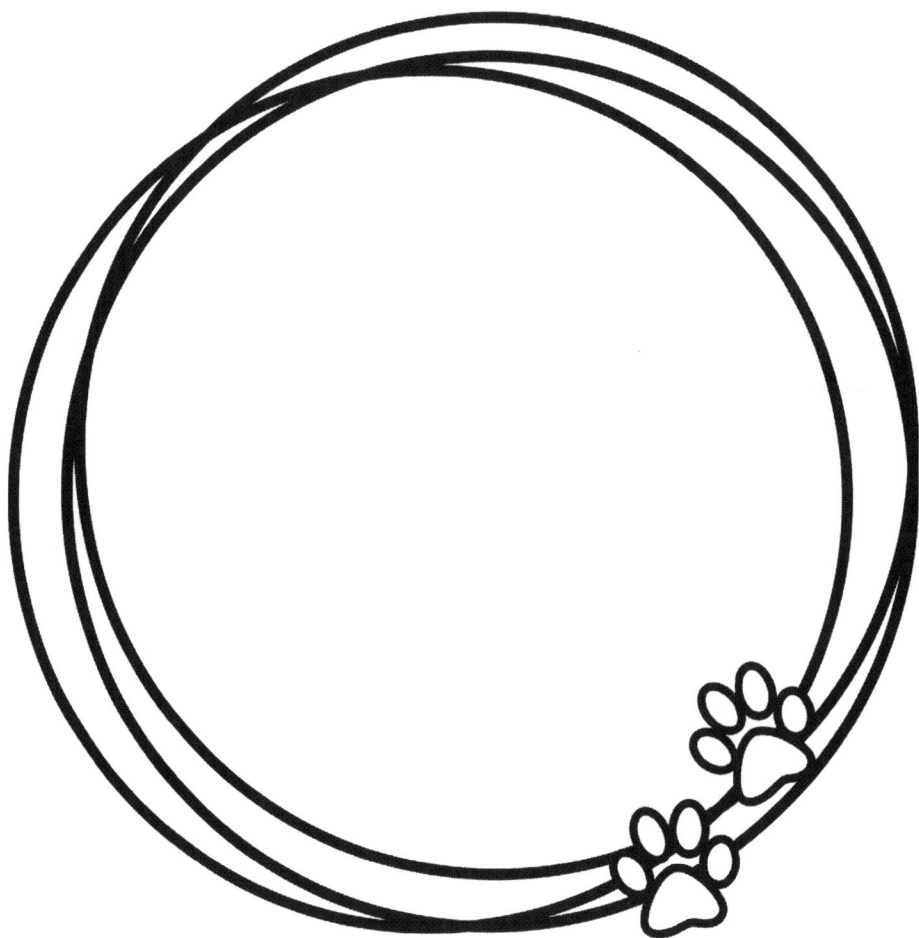

My New Puppy Journal

Remember When...

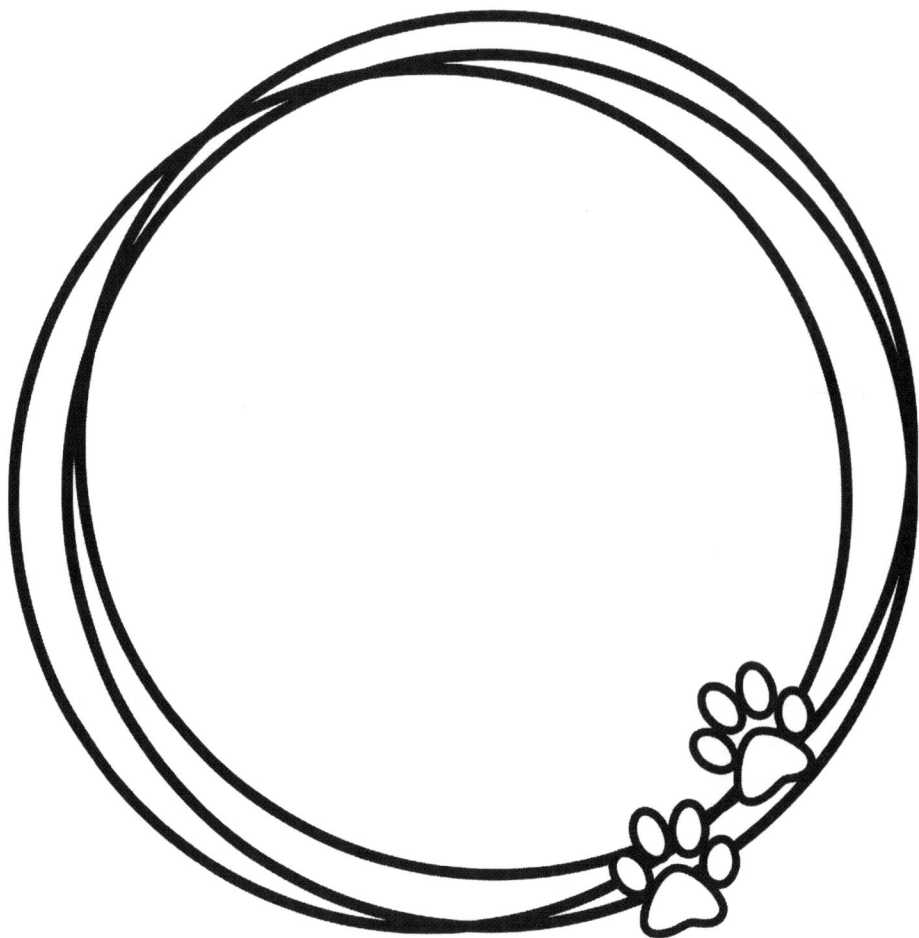

My New Puppy Journal

Remember When...

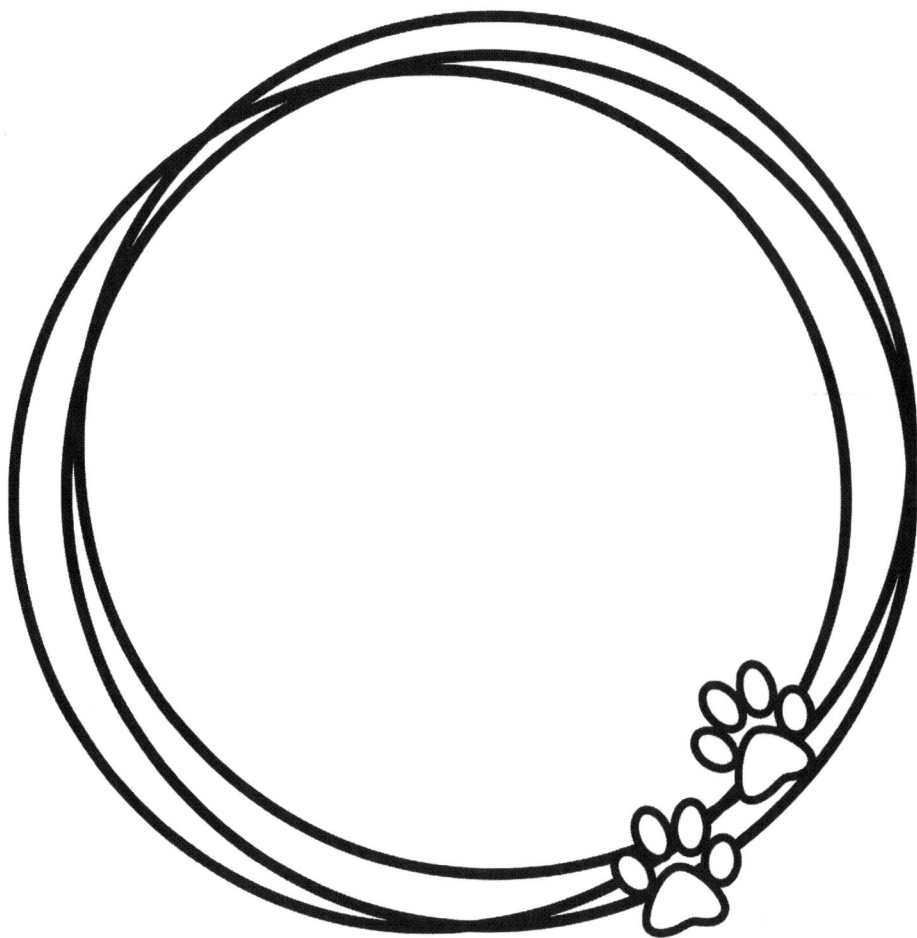

My New Puppy Journal

_____

_____

_____

_____

_____

_____

_____

_____

_____

_____

_____

_____

_____

_____

_____

_____

Remember When...

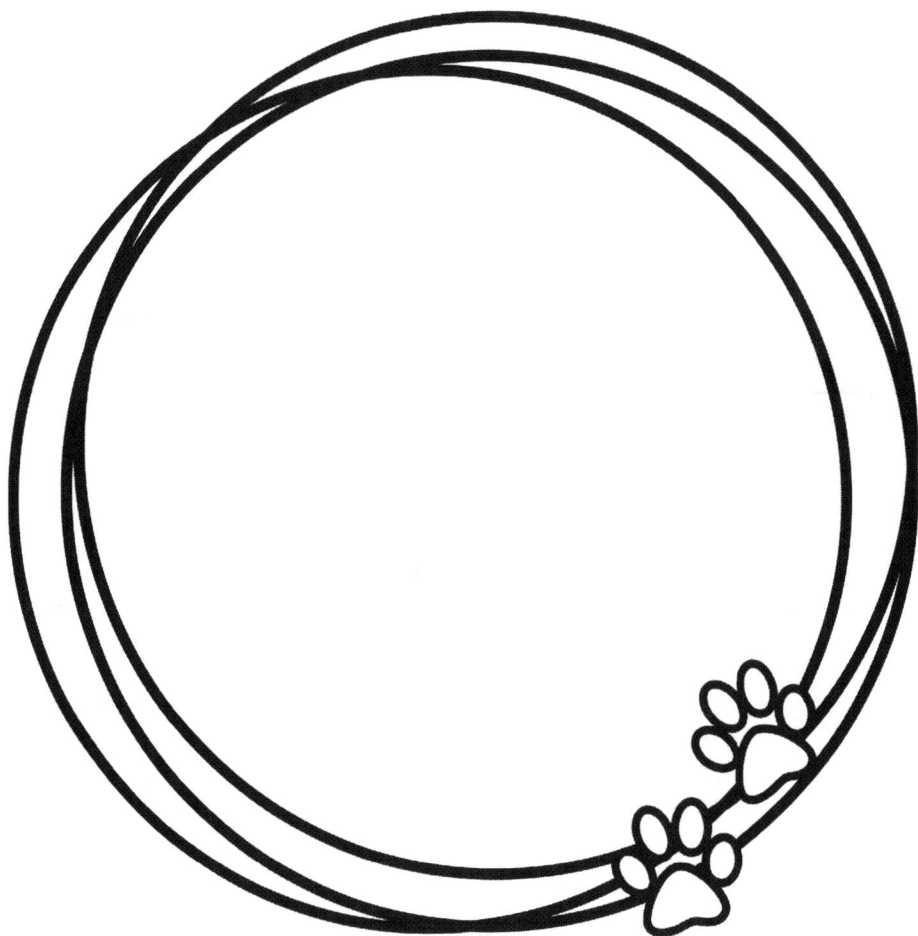

My New Puppy Journal

Remember When...

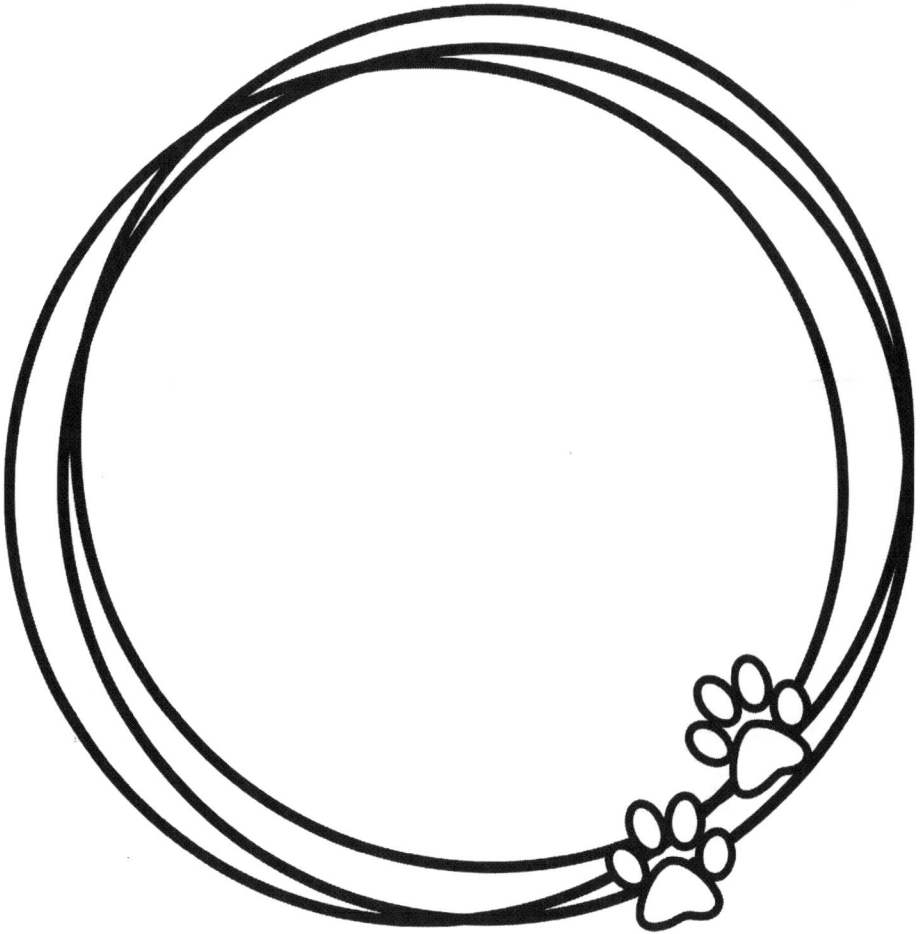

My New Puppy Journal

Remember When...

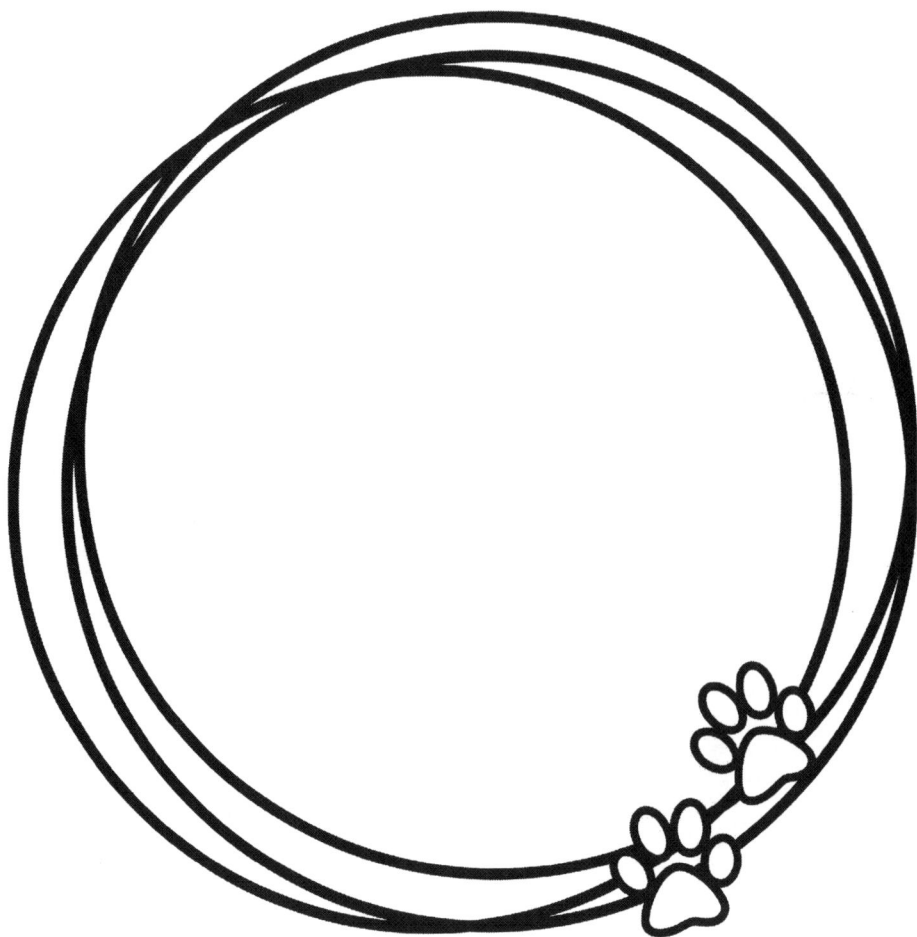

My New Puppy Journal

_____

_____

_____

_____

_____

_____

_____

_____

_____

_____

_____

_____

_____

_____

_____

_____

_____

_____

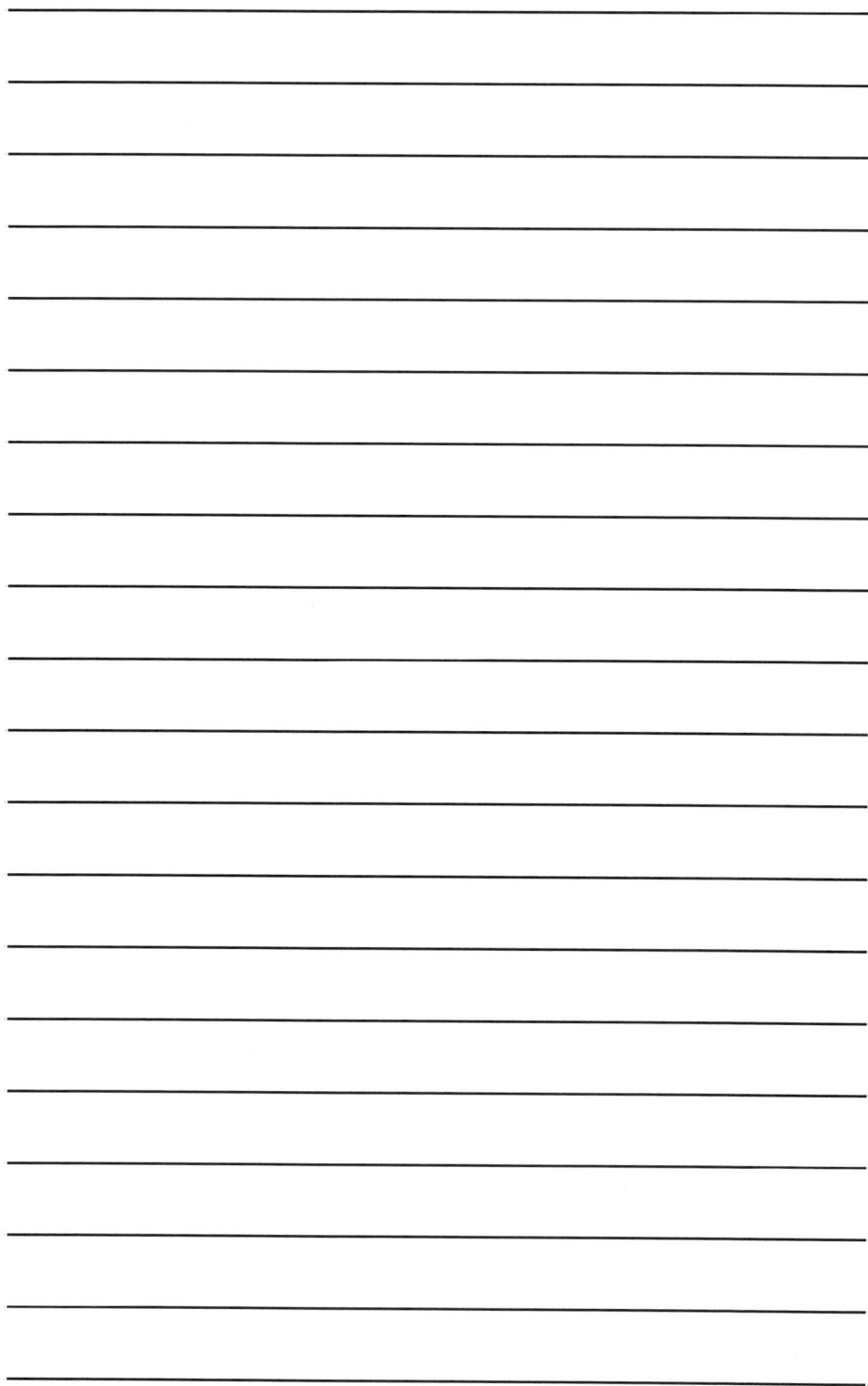

Made in the USA
Las Vegas, NV
13 January 2023